Take It

Take It

Joshua Beckman

WAVE BOOKS

SEATTLE   NEW YORK

Published by Wave Books
www.wavepoetry.com

Wave Books titles are distributed to the trade by
Consortium Book Sales and Distribution
Phone: 800-283-3572 / SAN 631-760X

This title is available in limited edition hardcover
directly from the publisher

Library of Congress Cataloging-in-Publication Data

Beckman, Joshua.
 Take it / Joshua Beckman. — 1st ed.
   p. cm.
 ISBN 978-1-933517-37-7 (pbk. : alk. paper)
 I. Title.
 PS3552.E2839T35 2009
 811'.54--dc22
                         2008039338

The author wishes to thank the editors of *Bat City Review, Big Bell,
Forklift Ohio, Fou, New American Writing, New York Quarterly, A Public
Space,* and *Satellite Telephone* as well as his family and friends.

Printed in the United States of America

9 8 7 6 5 4 3 2 1

FIRST EDITION

Wave Books 016

Contents

Take It

* * *

Dear Angry Mob,

Oak Wood Trail is closed to you. We
feel it unnecessary to defend our position,
for we have always thought of ourselves
(and rightly, I venture) as a haven for
those seeking a quiet and solitary
contemplation. We are truly sorry
for the inconvenience.

Signed,

      Ranger Lil

PS   Ofttimes as the day ends
        on a wet bed of yellow leaves
          or the sky densens gray and dark
    I am brought to imagine
      the growing disquiet
        in the hearts of my countrymen.

* * *

Through God's grace the little drops
came down on your head, and with one
sweep of an arm this earth was cleared.
Around my green soul there was a black circle
and an ashen world. Fitfully search the faces
for what is left and you will see each effect
of being, ghostly. The blood as it was given
by the heart and taken from the arm, the voice
if it is only air. I find, as in the animal world,
reminiscence disposes so quickly of its
architecture – so that a leaf, in dying,
might not fall or rot or float down the river,
that it might not find itself flattened between
the pages of a hymnal. Through God's grace
the little drops came down, and the spectacle
of human science blabbered on, just waiting
for something to witness up close.

* * *

I cannot help but by some sweet pill be devoured
she said – dancing and looking and helping people
with their thoughts – and then she had the baby –
and then you were running around and taking care of
everything – the lip, the thoughtful people. Financially
I'm made of music. Spiritually, I'm all full of cookies.
Great watchers and listeners and people with rings –
sit down beside your beloved for soon everyone
will be up and everyone will be asking questions.
The loud stuffing of people into corners with other people
and then the beautiful special people with skin kissing
each other. Why does the morning seem all draggy and alive?
There's no answer – just stand – and smarts – all curious.
Quiet is what the space said, quiet like tomorrow.

* * *

Cracked drags the callous enchantment of thought.
An ice collapse of snow upon. Way connecting way
of water. Engineers, who through inquisitive
deducement form. Those who scan the natural world
for need. A beautiful perfect horse etched into an
ashtray. Even the most fascinating, dynamic, and
wonderful people and things are, with distressing
regularity (near complete), mishandled and forgotten.
I feel now like I am saying sorry for something, when
what I am saying here is that the unknowing spirit is
greater than the knowing spirit, that no matter what
emboldened structure descends to stand before you
in its plan and fullness, you do not know what it is.

* * *

I don't long, I don't die, I don't await
the departure of those I love. As the origin
of a particular plant is sussed, so too
animals, people, their cities, and smaller things.
When you wonder on what I have become,
be just. No more great songs of satisfaction,
no more wailing upon the hill to the hillside.
Be kind, for trust is not addition and addition
is not acceptance and acceptance is not humility.
Simply put, we are a failed and ruined people
incapable of even silence. We are equal to nothing.
The earth given to us, we have lost even that.
Big eaters of America, I join you in your parade.
Let us be watched and let us be spoken of.
For today fascination is gone and even vanity
is undervalued. I have often misunderstood destiny,
I will misunderstand it no more.

* * *

Ousted by the neighbors from what had been
a perfectly comfortable dream, I wandered into
the hallway and fuck if there wasn't this kid
sort of straddling one of my houseplants,
pulling at its leaves, and the parents, they were
just standing there, looking at me! A small
car takes race with another equally small car
on a raceway in someone's living room.
I fall into such description as an oil baron
might speak of the world in a richer darker way,
but I am not an oil baron. A snow fell on
the mountains this week as if it were, as if
what it was doing was, anyhow, it's hard
to speak clearly on natural phenomenon.
My plan, as it stands, is to learn how to ski.
Pressing down on the snow I will be propelled.
"Hey man, where you going so fast?"

* * *

Expand if you will your mind over
the great oceans and through the deserts
and let your skull, like an umbrella
of stone, lower around it. The alligator
gets the bunny and the small bit of land
it was sitting on. From the night sky
comes a star that bounces off the ivory
tusk of an elephant onto a remote collection
of mushrooms and so endangers them.
When one is munching on some pizza,
one's jaw goes up and down. The tv said
the softball player and the baseball player
fell in love and made a baby. It said
they went to Hawaii for vacation and left
the baby under a banana tree, and then
that a banana fell on the baby (which was
funny) and scratched the baby's retina
(which was not funny). Through his
scratched and glistening eye he saw
the yellow bananas. Babies can't think,
but if they could, that baby would think:
They left me here like a baby soup in a pot
of bananas to get drunk with their new friends
from the airport (Tom and Christie) and
snort coke in their hotel room, but the baby

would never think: I am a news magazine
special, I am the banana that scares the
parents of other bananas.

* * *

Burnt by quiet reservation, as when
one animal waits for the barking of another
to go away – I have felt for some time
(since the picnic) that the branches
that form my enclosure are just too flimsy
and the leaves, while they can each be
counted on for their independent and colorful
expressions, are for all intents and purposes
transparent. What suspect and horrible fortune
is it that drags the lovers up the hill – a glass
of lake and pouncing on each other there.
Like a berry on a tooth of an evil-hearted boy.
That's not what I want to watch. Some ghostly
sailor ascended that he might tape up the sun –
gray, and so to be less remembered.

* * *

To leap and play and so to hear
your voice, to know what you have done.
Every day is the same. Some awkward
grip upon the friends who are never there.
No little wisdom entertains us when we are down.
When we are down we want fear and the acts of God.
How perfectly do you understand this? I don't
know that at all. I just look at my watch, I
stare at the snow, I lie around naked where
you can see. Sometimes I read or remember
how other people were to me. Poems should be
about clouds moving out of town and phone calls
should be about anything but time.
Might you agree to a truce?
No, I will never agree to a truce.

* * *

As a house is torn down with
the blowing of a trumpet, the soul
which has been stuck in the body
will soon be released – of certain
twisted things which only kneel
before themselves – that honey
colored cloud blew past – as in
season the heart lifts up – in bare
and unforgiving sleep – with
precious instinct floats that ruby
from your chest and so does glow
and live. A great head tipped off
the couch, like a little kitty's saucer
filled with something horrible. "Strung
up again with one's own ball of twine."
One private being gave birth to another.

* * *

The neighbors were going at it
with gas plungers again,
as if now, one hundred percent,
were the time to start making a dynasty.
While I, on the other hand, had just finished
consuming a day-old meat pie that tasted metallic and poisoned,
so rushing to the faucet I filled the first cup I could find
and that too seemed metallic and poisoned.
It only then occurred to me that some lazy Sunday ago
I had caught my boy watching an Agatha Christie
(instead of shining my trains), berated him, sent him off,
and wiggled myself into that cozy, warm chair
only to sack out fast, but not before realizing that
this, in fact, was how it might be done:
Leave a morsel sitting around and a cup beside it.
Swish swish swish and I guess the old man
just had one too many. "Nothing, you're getting
nothing," I cried. But the boy was nowhere to be found,
and the more I sobbed in the negative
the more that lady next door screamed yes.

* * *

That evening Ping felt so lonely.
Where is my child, he cried.
It was as if once there had been
a little bell hanging from his nose
that had amused him and now it
was gone. In fairy tales
one may go off into the forest
and become a monkey or plant
or something, but not in the
real world. In the real world
one is forced to put up posters
and feel awkward HAVE YOU SEEN
MY LITTLE GIRL? SHE WAS HERE
ONE SUNDAY WHEN NO ONE ELSE
WAS HERE It is like you had a friend
named Ricky who everyone, including you,
thought was charming and kind and
thoughtful and one day he was
never there again. But it is not
as though Ping wants you to see
his little child and bring her back,
it's just that he wants all the things
that have happened recently
not to have happened.

* * *

Yes, getting dragged by dogs on a sled
over an uninhabited ice bank is all I really need.
The stars. That quiet time "alone."
A bunch of diving birds.
Each thing was like the open mouth of my cave
and I was as a croquet ball on the endless
lawn of a great socialite, taking the perfect journey
through every gate. The dropped jaws,
the spilled lemontine drinks.
My thought then, being so close,
was of the pungent earth.
I rolled.
A magic relief, as in the story
when one finds oneself lost beneath
a canopy of fabulous tropical plants.
A fever of familiar people.
Each day I imagine the nourishing abstraction
of a hot sun. Each night the constellations
distract with proximity.

* * *

No list or illusive movement into being again
or later – that beautiful fitness of man – I know,
I'm sorry, but today it feels right – their rings
their shoulders, how they await their lovers
patiently. And we must care of nothing else
but this and knowledge. If it's fleeting don't
call it beauty and if it's love call it love.
So long have we forgiven ourselves an ancestry
that now we must attend to. Fragile us,
we said. Intemperate world, we said.
But here we are again among the mountains
and rivers, and what will we say now?
We deserve no more oceans, we deserve no more
banks, we deserve no more medication.
Athletically we live in this world and may we
speak no more of survival. I want to say, our gift,
but what, after that, would I say?

＊ ＊ ＊

Wild mysteries abound thy rocking plane, my love.
Take from me this great camping gear and small stove.
A fever about the very chest we kept our stuff in.
It gets hot, you remove your clothes and go in the water.
A book I have had in my possession for some time
relates the story of a girl obsessed with the finishing
of a miniature wooden boat. These fabric sails. Masts.
And I took from the story numerous visions of solitary
life, the awkward range of emotions sheltered in the
heart. A young enthusiast sunk in bottle glass.
This year was punctuated by a bare and restless viability.
In some uncomfortable manner, I lay in the garden,
atop the bloom and hollow,

                              "My back itches," I cried,
"Will you be a dear and find . . . oh yes, that's it."

                    In prairies, harbors, or above the humble
ripple of our lake, this sorrow I feel is baffling. Just
yesterday I accompanied the children to the blackberry patch
and like the resourceful mouse pulled thorns from the paws
of each one. I am sorry to write you such dreadful things
about my own self. How dumb. The growth of the world seems
to dye the fancy of a playful intelligence such assuming colors.
Forced floral regeneration. Ghost and pet.

* * *

It was as if her love had become
a big eye or some historical logic or
a religious particle lodged in the brain.
In the most costly services of a great society
one may find the allure of a benign intelligence.
I have hoped, since I was a child, to be surrounded by
a group of articulate characters who might
with gracious friendship provide
some essential entertainment

        as Aaron's

           which was a cane

      and then a snake

       and then a cane again

  great clouds

     of smoke from the forest

Itsy bugs amarch my naked legs

   in my beard, to burn

      as one might

       with one's eyes

I learned, but can no longer remember
with what dignity another's care imbues one.
You sit and pick the lice from my hair.
What sort of life is this.

* * *

The last bit of light made its way on
through the kind, through the caffeinated silence,
through the boot and voice. So you wish you had been
treated better, so I wish I had been treated better,
so we all wish we had been treated better,
but you are not the lovely feather
you make yourself out to be, stuffed
with white pills and the attention of others,
you're a lazy incompetent soul with a
beautiful way about you – which may, in fact
be just like a feather – so I'm sorry for saying
what I said, it's okay to want to be loved
and it's okay to want to be okay, but the next time
you call you better have something to say.
For in my house we are very tired, and being
tired makes us divisive, and you can do nothing with
a house divided, so don't even try, give up on trying.
A tap on the window, a rhythm of rain. We await
a better time and we believe a better time will come.
Judge, for I judge. Judge, for my household judges.
Weigh, judge, and discard while still these things have meaning,
for soon they will not, and then where will you be.

* * *

Time worn through as a great task or cloud
upon your countenance – this hand across this
face it cannot hide. Magically I shut your
eyes and you did sleep – glorious circus of fire
before your eyes and you did sleep – closed,
a blue that moves in sentimental tirelessness.
Have you listened to the things people say?
"I'm sweating" or "They chopped down that
tree." It is downright apocalyptic to be drawn
to your own safe place and to follow. Dream pray
thy home entunneled again with dignity, as a rat
washed up on a sorrowful beach. In your slicker
pocket there is a snack. I put it there.

* * *

A pulse asset with glorious visions,
the green river flown out of the cave,
an enormous hammer making from pulp
some distinct love (as, say, the Swiss
for their snow). A great discretion.
When the tenure committee said au revoir
I was, understandably, miffed.
Now, with you here and your little dog
I can lecture all night long, and then
scrape my teeth on your thigh. A candle
burned down my love – and that is only
God's anger – as it does rise in the morning
so it will set at night. Winter. The crème
de la crème of the forest. I treasure
every little thing you neglect for me.
In the quaint book of lessons, let
one more be recorded.

* * *

In Colorado, in Oregon, upon
each beloved fork, a birthday is celebrated.
I miss each and every one of my friends.
I believe in getting something for nothing.
Push the chair, and what I can tell you
with almost complete certainty
is that the chair won't mind.
And beyond hope,
I expect it is like this everywhere.
Music soothing people.
Change rolling under tables.
The immaculate cutoff so that we may continue.
A particular pair of trees waking up against the window.
This partnership of mind, and always now
in want of forgiveness. That forgiveness be
the domain of the individual,
like music or personal investment.
Great forward-thinking people brought us
the newspaper, and look what we have done.
It is time for forgiveness. Dear ones,
unmistakable quality will soon be upon us.
Don't wait for anything else.

* * *

Desert stylists were convening on
Port Washington for a vacation and
in a hotel room one sat me down
and began to discuss his wristwatch
as if it had a fundamental and symbolic
existence, a pattern of unified time
as little 2's march along or something.
I feel, no, I am certain, that right now
thieves are breaking into my apartment,
I must go. But this convinced him not.
Packs of boar were trampling in the
moonlight some needle or piece of shit
that the earth needed pushed into it.
God has made this hotel in his image.
The fluctuations of life. Yes. Yes,
I understand folly, we're the creatures
he explained that to.

* * *

Red, the want, the body, slowly
all perturbant drapes fall upon your cheek
and you are left here only to look and
to speculate on the first day of any one
thing. Oh world of pills, boats, and
polka dots, how you let me live, that's all.
A spinning love for some. A staring love
for some. An edifice. A comb. A kind
disquiet. The crew running back and forth.
Have you asked yourself how, with all we
know, we cannot enter the air as smoke
enters, or the lungs of others as smoke
enters. Have you asked yourself great
critical questions of form and matter, how
they will not spill into your day, or all
concentric circles eerily swimming
around you, as if you wish to ever
forget. On Thursday night you will
return from work to find me here,
and then a year, and then all those things
I have to do. A rose bag from which
the light will spill. And for some time
the light will be there and for some time
the empty bag.

* * *

Another pair of gilded transpirations
kept me happy all night – the bay aglow with revelers,
those shore hollow stones making home in your chest.
Cold waters that wash down such olympian quandaries
and sorrowful cascades set free. "Daniel, now hold that
cup carefully." That's the sort of thing mother
would say to me, the sun playing about the witch hazel
in the courtyard. With an emerald magnetism
the dew settles. I have been writing lately
on the grief of the body. I enclose
about my head memories and am in due course awoken.
In direct relation to the sun, wind, and rain
my apple tree produces.

* * *

Gold lesson like a pearl whose vocation
is being locked away, sweet as the day it was born.
Can you even stand the youthful voice of our pilot?
If we ever get to Salt Lake I want to buy that boy
a drink and give him some advice.
As a docent abstracted from his task
or a pine sunk in a valley
I imagine the supreme comfort with which
he tucks himself into bed and warmly dreams
of a God concerned only with weather.
By morning his measured thoughts are clear –
this misshapen landscape is but a challenge to us all.
A mountain, at the base of which was a town.
Your downturned lids.
I would be as patient as I could, and aware.

* * *

Dark and sparkled boot – beloved book from
which we learn – your intense eyes – I close
upon you now this hand – and north of here
the snow will land – as once you did gently
lift your pen from the letter – just what
have you said – tumbling over themselves –
I have seen them – no more jealous want or
ecstatic distance – a spell of holly, the
cloth wound round your body, gentlemen
lifting your bags as beside you they walk.
What will you think. Embrace this governed
love, and if it fits you clear – then count
your charms and draw your lover near. A little
fly meditates its way into a window – the
grove is soon too full – and what we believe
the outside world to be – is growth and growth
a substance of plainness. Architects of the world,
enclose me not tonight in your thoughtful rooms,
let me fall down the unbuilt hill, let me die
in the inconsiderate sun.

* * *

Drop the flower down your blouse
and set everyone on the bar to watch.
The still petal – the red ink – I wait here too.
The sweet storm knocks my boat around.
The snowy air. In our new upward spiral of time
it floats. All guessing gone sour, the golden age
of staring done. We do it over and over.
That one could put their smarts in such silly
articles – thoughtful, articulate, and perfectly kept.
Death to endurance and linen and that book
is a dumb block I'll lay my head on and each
miscarriage of justice – just salt – inside us
slowing us down – and then as you are coming to be
done, the guests, their gin and safety from the snow.
If for nothing else this – heat and fat and bodily
comfort. Elsewhere, as in her apartment, the dreamers
and the dressers unite in their dances,
the attractive neighbors on top of counters.
Customer meet the mirror, mirror meet the customer,
but before the dark meaninglessness of things
continues, let me cry this out of my system.
Lovely pill, one more time down my throat you will go,
and before long I'll be home – half real with people
on my tv. Swallow. Clean up. Return. And if I
keep doing it, that's what we call my life.

* * *

Some winter morning I struck off
on another indelicate journey:
a soul less full for willing calculation,
but let me tell you first how wonderfully
the light came through the side window
and left itself on my lover's torso:
through some upheaval of dust unrecorded
until now, an independent beam of light
set through the dead and shady apple tree
above the long grass yard, a downward
balance on the tiny window and dispelling
a brief static on the flattened belly there.
When I was a young man my father sat me
down – that glories may be mine,
life's spectacle embraced, he spoke
nigh sinful plumes of smoke and wizened
pets abounding leash behind – a little crack
on the head with his paper – "Son," he spoke
with singular and barbaric clarity, "Son,"
he repeated again, and from him then a speech
befitting the wayward traveler stilled only
by glory's momentum – so that he might stop
and assess the grand landscape before him –
"Only an ambitious God doth make such sights."
My own clairvoyant derangement returned.
"Out the door," I replied. "Yes, out the door,

my son." A cascade of paper on my little chest
and there in my lap it opened – but who would
believe I might even see what there was writ?
Reproachful souls do sleep as well lest thy canopy
of rest dost swell – the tempered bee, its field aglow –
the great solitary logics of the world as we do
now inhabit it – some lemon killed by a dog –
a beauty for all did move me and this, my friends,
was the worst: My lovely slept, as I said,
the sun with her, and I but another crimson sleeve
tumbled out into the neighborhood. First the light
and then the trees and then the buds and then
this unsophisticated rising earth and then
as a horror may visit you at any time,
the living dead, the dead insatiable.

* * *

When first I wrote I entrusted you with
a facile bit of self-complaint I now request
the return of. A simple gust of air breathed down
upon my house, adjusting my shutters (if you will)
and encapsulating me in that most sublime aspect of weather.
And lazing there I read your letter:

> "Well, I've given it a lot of thought,
> that marvelous stone wall and peach-shell construction
> are perfect for the back meadow, but I, for my
> own, all too personal reasons, must decline the offer.
> I wish you the best in these and other endeavors.
> Sincerely,"

Now you can imagine how this felt.
Well, it felt far more like a declaration to me.
A note dripping with concern is
really a slap in the face, or at least
that's how one can take such things.
But sense, if you will, the calmness of my tone.
I am as a cotton bug gently resting in the sun
aware only of his great fortune and bounty.
I can no longer deny the creator's will
in giving me this land.

– a great spread of fern and weed –

This dusty quiet car in which for years I slept.

It's quiet now alone, I see your dipping head

and angry jaw. Now comfort thy request.

I will, as to myself, be clear.

The house is mine.

I planted the flowers, which are mine.

The precociousness of any animal that wanders

onto my land will be mine.

Canny gloss of endless outward life.

Fixed will be my faucets, I recline.

* * *

You know how a heavy thought sits
 like a lump in you
  and in each and everyone you see.
 How with one's eyes
one cannot help but share such full concern.
  On Monday I was the most
overwhelmed – the way you
whipped around the hallway –
 cold soul held back
 and all about seemed
  full of only silence,
   and me too –
  the coming out of which was some
humorous description of an iced-over Russian town,
this fire in a little house, Geraldine closing her book
and nosing up to me in such rapture at them all
having been saved by their intelligence.

* * *

Good Lord Driscoll got the horses hitched
and then led us on to Guilford.
It has been a brilliant day.
My acquaintances were spectacular,
a sort of charming melange of pomp and cream.
Not to mention the pastry.
And the children with hoops and balls
in exceptional mimic of that insufferable woman
who always chases hornets around her shed.
As I was saying, one can feel certain of a given day
(often as that day is coming to a close)
that it has embraced itself with an openness
befitting the fortunes of existence.
Fine, and engrossed in one's own ways,
made close to the parts of one one might grow to miss.
The place spread about the walk, in grove and barn
the animals, and leaning back with delicate applause
all agreed. The finest cakes are made in abstract recognition
of other things we want, and yet we ate and eating well did sleep.
A thin stretch of light on the horizon, a mist on the fields,
a soft wind against the shutters, an awakening of insects
and children, the perfumed garden, the neighbors, the bell,
my creaking bed. That becoming appreciation of quiet.
Full of glory's expectant haze one might live.
This daring thoughtful place and then
the soldiers would return, and our town
would struggle once again.

* * *

One silver night the breeze puffed up our tent
so that returning to it we were stilled and frightened
and took cover behind the woodpile and watched
the dancing ash and held each other's hands.

Sweet and fragrant cold that descends
the named mountain to sleep here among the people
and never go away.

You have done all this
and now the frozen hair atop my head
your mocking cosmic light through cloud
and no bird all day.

* * *

What I have not claimed or executed on behalf
of my lover, I will this time for you.
Arrested image so caked upon my mind
that I felt stalked as a flower's stem
that must produce a bud and must
open – as, say, a falsely ingratiating presence
gets you to communicate in a dream as you
would otherwise never. I experience all
sorts of things, as if after a panning
yellow flash I find myself holding an object
with both my hands and trying to understand
exactly how to value it – the process of
which is like some horrible draining
judgment, ceramic and the size of a
hollow pear, incoherently coupled with my
self as the hardened crater and the plane
that will not crash. The dart is more
ingenious than violent. The coffin, too.
At approximately the same time all of
the flesh will have rotted and receded
from the bones, and some tribe finding us
will recognize our forearms or ribs
as the makings of a musical instrument or pattern plate
for passionate expressions like the ones my
stupid tongue does fail to produce.

* * *

My life at Nettle Abbey was as you might expect.
Thrown from one's horse onto someone else's horse
was as good as it got. Being the sort who really
does appreciate an awkward compliment, I waited
there like I might never be woke again, but in no time
I was heard to howl and bemoan my wretched cause.
How often might one get water splashed in one's eyes
before the salty crust on one's forehead becomes a part
of one's expression? I do wish I were not so stubborn,
for I would much prefer to return home to you
and fill that little bowl with milk myself. But, my dear,
do not be deceived – a hare might think he does fine
to find himself asleep a lettuce patch, but it
is certainly there where the laziest owners of the
laziest hounds do suck their pipes. And so, like my
companions, I dream not of the tender head and leaf
but of the spastic dismantling of spirit between
the teeth of my enemy.

* * *

I am a lazy caterpillar on a snow crumb,
the warm light from the sun in my world.
I have a beetle friend who has wrapped
a leaf around himself and gone to bed.

"In the daytime?"

"Why, yes, many of us here
are like that. We find rest
and calm in the bustle and
warmth, our bodies rejuvenated
and focused."

Hoisting crates into the truck, Lou, the shopkeep, missed me
completely. Curled around the apple stem, I was thinking
of all the things I would never ever do again.
                                        I have broken
the skin with my front teeth and the tangy juice
pools around them and onto my tongue.
I flex my hundred legs in pleasure and still
my mind rebuts – job job job job job job
job job job

* * *

Whistling into your picture and finding naught
but the lonely still so afraid. Before long we
will head above ground, the spun thread of all
that lies gently upon your leg will prepare for the
lift and glare that wakes you up. Only the done and
the sad must be sorry, only the dead spot in your
brain where the blood silently pools. Let us to the
Carolinas go – and there rest in that moveless sun –
no more nearness and worry – no more undeclared
weakness. My ankles are crushed, my eyes, when God
knelt down in front of those children it was already
too late. Yesterday in your queer drunken state you
went and when you called – such shallow charms for
will we cannot go – you said it so simply – that lace
on your leg, and those who do so sew such things
in hope of keeping them.

* * *

So untrue my firm countrymen, so untrue.
Your reckless hellos and your gurgling sorrows –

        clasped in each other's arms.

I direct you to the grand panorama that God has built –
some hundred years ago over that ridge they came,
strong planks smashed into dirt

            my rocker rocks on pounded earth

In my lap a quilt is lain.
Child, ask your brother to go check the sundial.
The Beckman clan calls for the death of another animal,
and I need finish my sewing by nightfall.

* * *

This playful dance.
The great cornfields in harvest.
What monstrous impulse allows us turn on those we love.
I went sliding down the hill on a block of ice.
Vague home, a bridge, your lover's sad hanging bangs.
Little children with little noses and little lips.
That a body could fold up and sleep.
I cut that tree into a thousand pieces
and burned it all winter.

As some timely drop
    an orange descended
      from a branch
    into my hands –
and in front of me it stayed.

These are the times when one's attention
      is taken by beautiful things
    most fully, I imagine, in loss.

* * *

To eat the little white pill and
walk around as air, I enter,
with my fingers, your hair, and so
am half barrette, half smoke leaving
lips. The garden. The glassed-in
station. A balloon lowered as a flower
and a flower as light in water.
So simply to bounce around and ask
something of everything – given over
to work and faith – it is to the people
of my life I quietly speak: Go by,
kill pain, and accept. A glance
along the shoulder of what it is
you want. Patter, the finger. Shutter,
the thigh. Through each of us something,
a shower, the time.

* * *

My square rock is a piece of art. I put
it on the sill like it itself is a sill
and then put something on top of it so that
it may be alone, like a tangerine on some
thing which is bright and attracts attention
and may even be taken and eaten and yet still
is somehow able to be.

                I expect
you can't yet tell how wonderful all this is,
and furthermore I expect that this absence
of wonder is my own fault. Okay then, let me
try again: Once upon a time a cabbage sat beneath
a lamp and did not grow and did not shrink
and did not perceptibly change, and while this
may be an exceedingly average and common trait
for a cabbage, it is, as a description, plagued
with inaccuracy. I think we can all agree that a
cabbage, having been taken from the garden,
remains very mostly a living thing.

                Our bright green
life together is so confusing. I hold you sometimes
and make you happy and then sometimes you walk
around the living room and are unhappy. People
who love each other are supposed to have some
magical way of understanding each other.

                Passed out,

my mouth was agape, but my heart and my
blood and my breathing systems soldiered on.
You poured a little drop of water into me, that
I might feel better, and it became a bead and traveled
all the way down my throat and out my toe and oddly,
oddly, neither of us noticed.

* * *

I am aware of the great numerological mysteries
that have taken place in the British Isles over
the past thousand years. The first, and certainly
the most implausible, is the count of birds on
William the Earl of Pembroke's shield, found
in Westminster Abbey. If one, in visiting
the church and seeing the shield firsthand,
begins to count from the upper right, one finds there
only six birds, and yet if one counts from the upper left
one finds nearly ten. This mystery is further re-
inforced by the countless varied illustrations
undertaken since its creation (circa 1296) and maintained
in our present day by a strict prohibition of photography.
The second great mystery, commonly known to all Scots,
and often thought to be a national ruse by tourists,
is the annual adjustment of leaves on the Scottish Pea Flower
(ironically, from seven in even years to six in odd).
Countless charming mythologies have been created to
explain the fascination, and nearly every county holds
firm to its own. Finally, and most recently, in Belfast's
main hospital, a varied pitch of simultaneous cries
from a team of visiting nurses in a celebratory waiting room
constructed together to form a pressure on the chest of a dying
boy from Croom, so that he was near instantly revived by the
ecstatic tangle of their voices, his stunned family moveless of
tears. When one begins to consider such a range of effects
in collaboration, one is brought to a deeper cosmic certainty,

and from there to a profoundly thirsty disposition, wondering
what foolish scientist creates a lamb that already exists, what
foolish scientist wakes in the night bent on the destruction
of anything.

* * *

So then in yellow structures
of glass and concrete and wood, yes, like
the floating junk, river patch, house, red,
light, knock, drag, "No, I'm not here.
I don't even know why this is where you
came looking for me." One teardrop-shaped
hole next to another teardrop-shaped hole
and round like a daisy with a center, which
is how, through my aluminum wall, I see.
All light moves at angles, everyone knows
that. The colors of their petals and stems.
It is said that floating plants are the most
"intelligent" – the beings landing on them
from above being convinced of their strength
and opacity by the beings below nosing into
them, and likewise the beings below made
nervous. Cathy would say, you're an idiot,
no light gets through no hole without being
stopped. The plant that falls is the plant
that falls. The plant that floats is the plant
that floats, and on. Jewels are the exhibition
of these very systems at their most calm,
which is why they are exalted, and then
flora, and then us, so frantic that we barely
seem to be systems at all.

* * *

The king who only the buffoon can
make fun of with impunity.
The king who only the buffoon can
make fun of with impunity.
The king who only the buffoon can
make fun of with impunity.
My dressing room was like
a pharmacy and after the show
I would always go there and
stare at the silly picture
of the girl and the corvette
until someone would knock
and then I'd say, "Is all my
makeup off?" and they'd lie
and say yes.

* * *

To get ready I was watching *Hope From Comfort*,
the seventies cult classic about the assistant
zookeeper who falls into an "alternate universe"
populated by crudely geometric forms and, despite
the hero's pathological belief otherwise, completely
uninhabited by the living. The movie, even with
its unambitious production values, reccurred in my
waking and sleeping dreams with alarming regularity.
Like much other science fiction of the time, it is
almost fully dependent on an internal narration.
When there is a mountain it is a paper maché mountain
and the fog, which that first day baffles him
with fear, is most probably from the director's
own pipe. And yet, if one were to think objectively,
every attempted reenactment of human emotion and
experience is equally crude. Having basically not
sobered up before the interview, I explained it like
this: The great and deserved accolades that your
characters have received over the past few years
continue to fall in a thick carpet around them, lulling,
cooling, and setting at risk the entire series.
With all due respect, Theodore needs to be more moved
by the constant attention of his son, Dahlia's parodic
surging hormones should be more alarming to her (and
near paralyzing to her boyfriend), Wick acts the same
when he is alone and when he is with others, and on
and on I went, and as I came to the end they tried to

stop me but they couldn't stop me, I could see it –
the entire town, the neighbors, the family, and
then here's the cherry I said, "Pets. Do any of you
have pets?" because Lulu could own this show if you
just let her do something but scratch and beg.
Asshole, they thought, as they waved goodbye.
But some thankful cat god was licking my face with
its perfect tongue, and I knew I had said the right thing.

* * *

Constance,

I have left for the Orient. While I recognize that
this may be seen as yet another admission of my bold
and fruitless temperament, I am, at present, little
concerned with such things. When had we once spent
a lovely wistful day by the seashore? When had we . . .
Oh, it's of no use, the Queen wants spices and so
spices I am off to find. Perchance more pleasant
to perch worked upon a forest rock looking into a
pool. But still, how clever one must be to find
oneself on a coin. The clouds were filling with
red light. A religious wind was crashing against the
rocks. Straw bonnets floated ashore. Rush, cried
the captain, and from the air a chorus on the blind
passage of souls into the ease bellowed out.
A vein of some precious metal.
But it was not to be. The tide returned us home
just fine, and this is but the explanation I arrived at.

* * *

Simple the full sail, the half-full sail,
your crew skittering across the floor –
How was the day, you ask, is that
what turned you brown? And then
to be bored and healthy.
                    A man sending lines
off a building, the down down there
in the dirt, your empty arguable clarity
        and that fuck with his finger
in the terminal.
                    Oh pornographic certitude
of the uncivilized, rolling over each other
like puppies.

Listen to who walks beside me
Watch the day begin its fading
You who sit and wait for lightning
Leave the empty action be

Boom, or alight on ice
with your very own pickax.

Dear Family, our enemy
weakens, mornings come early, I have grown
comfortable, I will miss the roses again
this year, say hi to Phoebe, I hope she
finally got that pool. If everything's not

wicked, then unimaginably glorious is every
piece of rubbish. Providence. Remembering
the house and then (later) seeing the house
burned down. It's like every bastard here
brought pictures. I am glad you are well.
I am sorry to not have written sooner.
My life is a dream. When they ask, say,
His life is a dream.

* * *

Dark mornings shown thy mask
made well thy visage and voice
rolling over and hearing some perfect
sweetness that one broad soul poured forth
again in happy countenance and ancient word

           my city cold
             for me, my nature
               lost

             come back

         sallow soft and colorless
        thy dreams repent

  as:

The whole family
each with his own

           "Now, sweet child, we must
           kiss winter goodbye, and so too
           your furs."

She clutched the puppy to her breast.

"Not little Bobby, father."

"Yes, my darling, little Bobby as well."

And this, as she ought, was how Gretel remembered summer – a constant giving up of things and people.

* * *

Tinsel's cold stove, first like
rotten sex and then like a drop
of nothing that creates a fog
before your eyes. This dead winter
morning, let's just say I indulged
in a little bit of overdirecting.
The extras were to be quiet and
gritty as Texan bartenders – No,
no, I think I said, soft and
essential as raindrops made of
baby cloth. Listen, people,
when Tinsel sings his sad number
I want half of you to be rays of light
and the other half to be beams. Remember,
it's more than him just getting his
heat turned off, his life is really
a gully huck of dumb suds reflecting
from his shoes like he's got sausages
stuck in those things, and if the chorus
doesn't recognize his subtlety, than no one
will. And then, in usual flourish, he
walked in and cried, "Mon frère, you
shake like a tractor at a samba lesson."
The gall! But, showing my personal
fortitude and businesslike grace, I said,
as part of a raffle I won this flight,
and I guess I just thought it would

do you some good, Tinsel.
Take it, I said, get out of town. We'll
work on the voice-overs while you're gone
(which was never going to happen).
But it didn't matter. When he returned
it was completely different. His mind
was a calm reluctant piece of coral,
and his words spread out as tankers making
their way from Japan, weeks between them,
and yet in the wide ocean still forming a line,
which was absolute glory for ending a movie.
Total constancy and incontrovertible snow.
The Times said, touching.

* * *

Carefully I placed the register on the counter
and began to thumb through. When one recognizes
a ghostly squeal from but tacit reminiscences, one is near,
as they say, the deep end. If I was to convince you of
the quality, nay, the qualities of my work here at the
hotel, I began, what would my first step be? My arms
were jangling and elevated beyond principle, which
is when Kyle showed up. Like a crab, and being
from Maryland to boot, Kyle had a fondness for
the flourishes of proximate relation (like ants) and
it was interests such as these that acted upon me
a growing trust and affection for Kyle. Galloping
about the teahouse he would let his theories grow
in light relation to the near variety of inhabitants there
and return with an exquisite new arrangement for his
curiosity. When one peruses any average metropolitan
area, one cannot help but to notice a profound disintegration
in (what a more conservative man might call) our social
fabric. My goodness, that woman's coffee cup is cracked
and yet look how she purses her lips around its rim.
Cross yourself, he would say, a wind of evil just blew
through this place or, I noticed that you tucked your
shirt in today. Dropped into the ether acre, he fondled
the register. Lou Francis, how long was he here for, and
Pearl Sands, what a fabulous name. You know, if you
don't (at that moment he saw clearly the whiteness and
rigor of my choppers, gleaming), if you don't give up

this post immediately, I will be forced to venture off,
taking with me this gross little view of you I just had.
Early that morning, in dread, I had been considering
this very possibility, so sharpening my counter and
returning the register to its shelf, I silently agreed.
It is possible and common events such as these that I
speak to you of today, nothing more. The deft accumulation
of affection between friends, and what power it might have.

* * *

Then then the first cooled surface
of labor, like a table of smoke
above a fire, above which is light.
A bellows, the mysterious function
of sand, tact of great stone, the giant's
tooth, as when you stare out over a landscape
seeing some destroyed tree or rock where
it seems not to have been before, where
in fact, nothing seems to have been before.
I placed my head on the pillow, where an
abstract chemistry appeared to explain its objects.
I put the telephone on my chest and
crushed it with a rock and then ate the insides.
From our car we saw the coyote getting closer.
What they say is: These poor creatures have been
domesticated beyond their ability to successfully
reason the dangers that approaching the road hold for them.
Continue in your cars at a thoughtful pace. Our park is
full of a variety of natural curiosities which thrive,
unharmed by your attention.

* * *

I am made of butter, I am wrapped in gold,
I am forgotten as a frialator forgets a haddock,
and then I tell my sweet love that I want to spill
coffee all over her bottomside, and she tells her friends,
so they take her to the country where they all
go for walks and play honesty games.
                                    I sing a tune
from a great heavenly road about a pricker
stabbed into the side of an animal. If my Irish gang
was done terrorizing the neighborhood, Colin,
our leader, would lie down in the yard atop a
photographic canvas, and by the sun he would be
put to sleep and by the sun too he would be
reproduced – in silhouette, his curved arm and
finger would point to some mean, ravaged person
and then his out-turned leg being like a mountain,
and his cock like a beetle or a cricket, and his hair grass.
When my love returned she lay her body on the
photographic canvas and the saturation of light
took its effect. Lo, and before long we had all
tried our bodies, forming a great evident
contrast, and then a transcendent gravitational
ease of process, and then she would rise and
stand there with the others – a temporary address
of graph and compass, and then someone else would
lie down, and then someone else. Grip friends,

for the world a growing display of signs is,
and I imagine, will continue to be.

* * *

Roger called for another long beach of grasses
to be laid before him, and when it was done, for
pheasants, and when the pheasants had been brought,
he called for his gun, which was to be some wood-
handled replica of another gun, and when it came
he asked that small, pink-faced children of a
Northern European variety be placed around it
in a semicircle, protecting it and him from the
brutish yet kind-hearted thief he had called for
earlier and who had come and lunched and waited
(in the foreground), and when he asked for the sun
and the sun's rays and for the unexplained magic
of photosynthesis that would grow the grasses high,
he asked also for a hat so that whoever might come
looking for him in the tall grasses could, by the
sight of the hat, find him, and when this came he
felt relieved as if that very last thing had been
the most sensible. But it was in this exact landscape
that the mossy box of bullets sat, a magnifying glass
leaned up against it, thinking, "Wrong, wrong, wrong.
No one ever knows what to wish for."